Australian Animals

Kangaroos

Sara Louise Kras

raintree
a Capstone company — publishers for children

Raintree is an imprint of Capstone Global Library Limited, a company incorporated in
England and Wales having its registered office at 264 Banbury Road, Oxford, OX2 7DY –
Registered company number: 6695582

www.raintree.co.uk
myorders@raintree.co.uk

Edited by Jessica Server
Designed by Charmaine Whitman
Picture research by Jo Miller
Production by Katie LaVigne
Originated by Capstone Global Library Ltd
Printed and bound in India

ISBN 978 1 4747 7553 3 (hardback)
22 21 20 19 18
10 9 8 7 6 5 4 3 2 1

ISBN 978 1 4747 6045 4 (paperback)
23 22 21 20 19
10 9 8 7 6 5 4 3 2 1

British Library Cataloguing in Publication Data
A full catalogue record for this book is available from the British Library.

Acknowledgements
We would like to thank the following for permission to reproduce photographs:
Alamy: Juergen Sohns, cover; Dreamstime: Kazzadev, 11, Sain Alizada, 9; iStockphoto:
CraigRJD, 13, 19, MaXPdia, 5; Minden Pictures: Yva Momatiuk and John Eastcott, 17;
Shutterstock: deb talan, 7, Jeremy Red, 15, Nicole Patience, 1, Pawel Papis, 21
Design elements: Shutterstock: Pyty (map), oksanka007

Every effort has been made to contact copyright holders of material reproduced in this
book. Any omissions will be rectified in subsequent printings if notice is given to the
publisher.

Contents

Living in Australia

Australia has mammals that can hop at a top speed of about 44 kilometres (27 miles) an hour. They are kangaroos. They use their big back legs to move fast.

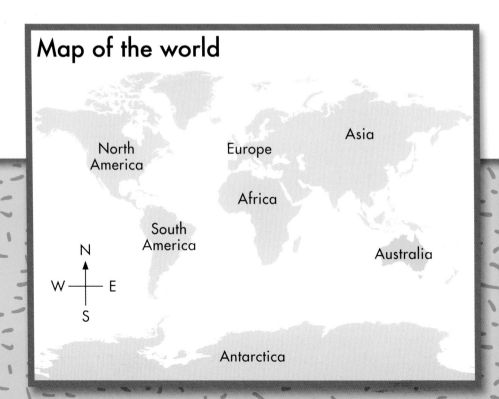

Map of the world

North America
Europe
Asia
Africa
South America
Australia
Antarctica

There are different types of kangaroo. The largest is the red kangaroo. Some kangaroos live in Australia's hot bushlands. The rest of them live in forests and grasslands.

Kangaroos live all over Australia.

Map of Australia

grey
kangaroo

Legs, paws and tails

Kangaroos have two long back legs that are made for jumping. If a kangaroo needs to get away from a predator, it can jump 9 metres (almost 30 feet) in one leap!

Kangaroos' front paws have sharp claws. They use their claws to dig in the ground to look for water. They also use their claws to fight with other kangaroos.

Kangaroos have big, thick tails.

They lean back on their tails to rest.

Kangaroos also whip their tails up

and down when they hop. This

helps them to keep their balance.

Eating and drinking

Kangaroos eat grass. They can last a long time without water. Eating grass gives kangaroos some of the water they need.

Growing up

Kangaroos belong to a group of animals called marsupials. Marsupials have pouches on their bellies. Kangaroo babies grow in their mothers' pouches. When they are born, the babies are about the size of a jellybean.

Young kangaroos are called joeys. Joeys stay in their mothers' pouches for up to 10 months. Adult kangaroos live for around 8 to 12 years in the wild.

Staying safe

Some kangaroos live in groups called mobs. One male kangaroo is the leader. He watches for predators and keeps the mob safe.

Glossary

balance to keep steady and not fall over

bushlands dry part of Australia where trees and shrubs grow

joey young kangaroo

mammal warm-blooded animal that has a backbone and hair or fur; female mammals feed milk to their young

marsupial animal that carries its young in a pouch

mob group of kangaroos that live together

pouch pocket-like flap of skin

predator animal that hunts other animals for food

Find out more

Books

Baby Animals in Pouches (Little Pebble: Baby Animals and Their Homes, Martha E.H. Rustad (Raintree, 2018)

Kangaroos (Pebble Plus: Meet Desert Animals), Rose Davin (Raintree, 2017)

The Story of the Kangaroo (Fabulous Animals), Anita Ganeri (Raintree, 2016)

Websites

This website has lots of fun facts about kangaroos:
www.sciencekids.co.nz/sciencefacts/animals/kangaroo.html

Find out more about marsupials at this website:
www.dkfindout.com/uk/animals-and-nature/mammals/marsupials/

You can also find out more about marsupials at:
kids.britannica.com/kids/article/marsupial/353437

Comprehension questions

1. What do kangaroos eat?

2. What do you think is the kangaroo's most powerful body part? Why?

3. Where do baby kangaroos live?

Index